FIVE THOUSAND SUFFRAGETTES SING ETHEL SMYTH'S "MARCH OF THE WOMEN" ON THE STEPS OF THE US CAPITOL IN 1914.

Rise Up
with a
Song

For everyone who believes in a wider tomorrow for us all, and especially for Kayla and Charlotte, who inspire me with their grit every day. —D.W.

BUSHEL
& PECK
BOOKS

Text copyright © 2022 by Diane Worthey
Illustrations copyright © 2022 by Helena Pérez García

Published by Bushel & Peck Books, a family-run publishing house in Fresno, California, that believes in uplifting children with the highest standards of art, music, literature, and ideas. Find beautiful books for gifted young minds at www.bushelandpeckbooks.com.

Type set in Jacob Riley, Calder Script, and Calder Dark.

Photo credits: Experiential Orchestra and Chorus (Allison Stock); endpaper visuals (US Library of Congress); front cover icon (Shutterstock.com/Anastasiia Veretennikova).

Bushel & Peck Books is dedicated to fighting illiteracy all over the world. For every book we sell, we donate one to a child in need—book for book. To nominate a school or organization to receive free books, please visit www.bushelandpeckbooks.com.

LCCN: 2022940426
ISBN: 9781638191315

First Edition

Printed in China

10 9 8 7 6 5 4 3 2 1

Rise Up with a Song

THE TRUE STORY OF
Ethel Smyth,
SUFFRAGETTE COMPOSER

Diane Worthey, Illustrated by Helena Pérez García

In 1867 England, a girl spoke when spoken to, learned needlework, and glided when she walked.

But Ethel Smyth marched to a different beat.

Under the barnyard fence
to ride Fairylight the pig.

Over the garden wall
in search of forbidden fruit.

And through the family graveyard
in the dark of night.

Governesses came . . .

. . . and left.

None lasted long with Ethel. But at twelve years old, as she contemplated her next disobedient stunt, something magical stopped her in her tracks.

The new governess, a graduate of Leipzig Conservatory, sat at the piano, her hands dancing across the keys. Golden strains of Beethoven sonatas floated up, down, and all around.

The music pulsed with life! It didn't stay in one place. The music soared!

From that moment, Ethel's desire **burned**. She spent hours each day writing music to accompany her favorite poems.

Her piano teacher, Mr. Ewing, was enamored of her work.

"She's headed for a career in music!"

he told her parents.

"Utter nonsense!"

said her father.

Ethel's father forbade her to pursue a career in music.
He thought women belonged at home, not on the stage.

Ethel locked herself
in her room and
refused to come
out. Not even for
dinner!

Her father tried to break down the door to her bedroom.

But the door didn't budge.

Neither did Ethel. At last, her father relented. She was free to study music.

At Leipzig Conservatory, women conformed to society's rules of genteel behavior.

Not Ethel.

She taught her friends how to jump over tables, chairs, and even fences!

Classmates sat at their pianos to write music.

Not Ethel. She found inspiration off the beaten path— up a mountain and under the trees.

The whoosh of the wind, the trill of the lark, and the rush of water in mountain streams became notes that marched across the page . . . moving, singing, roaring.

People told her she wouldn't succeed as a composer because she was a woman. Her friends Johannes Brahms, Pyotr Ilyich Tchaikovsky, and Edvard Grieg could sign their full names to their works.

Not Ethel.

Sometimes her music was only accepted for publication if she removed her first name from the work.

Operas.

Symphonies.

Choral works.

Musicians performed her music, and her fame grew and grew.

With her success, she no longer had to pretend to be a man. Proudly, she signed her music:

"Ethel Smyth."

But some orchestras refused to perform her music when players realized she was a woman.

Other times, publishers simply refused to pay Ethel for her work.

"Not fair!"

cried Ethel.

Music wasn't the only place where women were shut out.
Women were excluded from places of power.
They couldn't even vote in elections!
Ethel was tired of women being silenced.

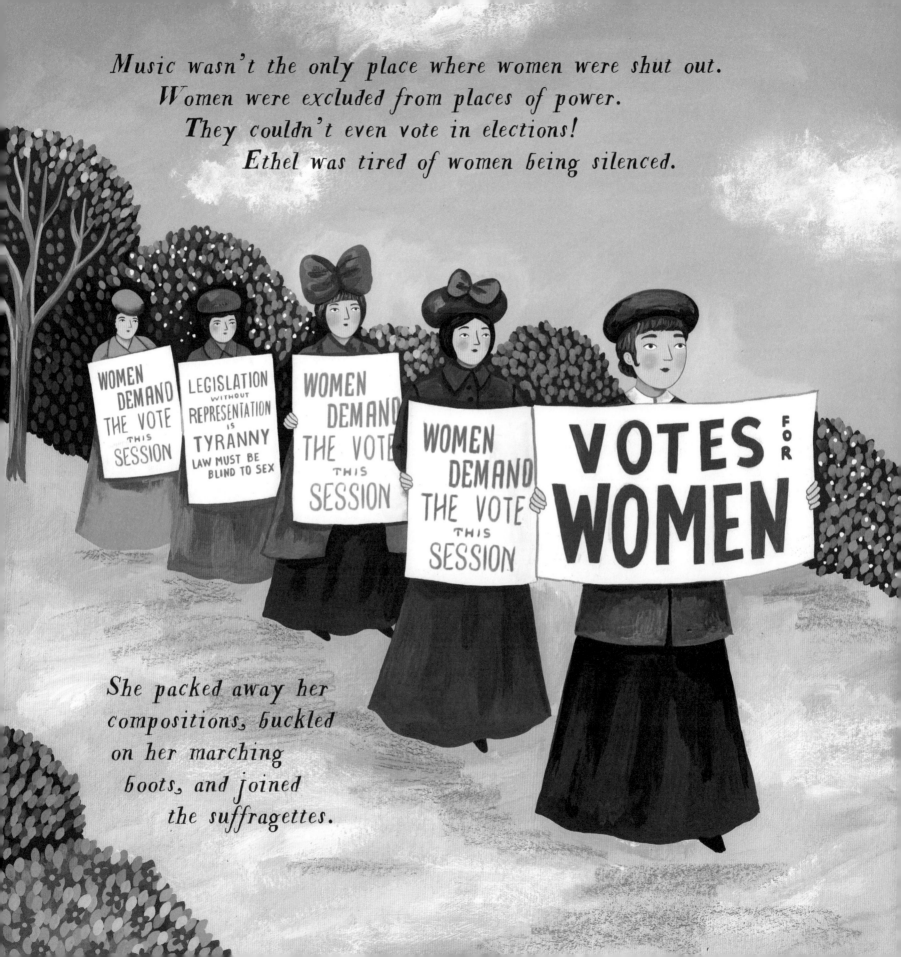

She packed away her
compositions, buckled
on her marching
boots, and joined
the suffragettes.

Ethel and her friends marched and chanted through the streets of London.

DEEDS NOT WORDS

SOCI...
AND
...CA...

VOTES

No one listened to their pleas.

"Not fair!"

said Ethel.

The women needed a battle cry that
would ring through the streets.
Ethel set pen to paper.
Notes flooded the page.

"March, march, up with your Song!
Cry with the wind, for the dawn is breaking

"March, march, swing you along
Wide blows our banner and hope is waking!"

For months, day in and day out, Ethel led the women in song as they boldly marched in pursuit of justice. But nothing changed. Women were still barred from the voting booth.

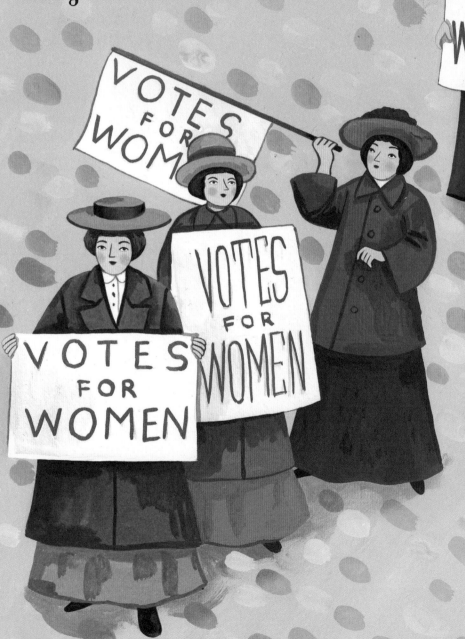

Ethel had a **daring** idea. What if she could bring attention to the women's pleas by going to prison? A famous woman composer locked behind bars would certainly gain attention.

She tapped a policeman on the shoulder to make sure he was looking. Then, she *hurled* a rock straight through the cabinet minister's window.

Glass tinkled to the ground.

Holloway Prison brimmed with suffragettes. They broke the law to bring attention to the plight of women. The suffragettes were only allowed to meet freely during certain hours.

Some women danced.

Others squeezed animal sculptures out of bread.

Ethel spent her free time organizing the prisoners in **song**.

One such morning, a
crowd of women gathered
outside in the courtyard.
Where was Ethel?

Suddenly, the women heard the steady **rap** of a baton from high above.

As they gazed skyward, Ethel leaned gallantly out her cell window, toothbrush in hand, and beat time with a **frenzy**.

As dawn broke, hundreds of prisoners followed Ethel's toothbrush baton as they sang and marched in step around the courtyard. Ethel's "March of the Women" carried on the wind, through the prison yard, and to the streets of London.

"Comrades, ye who have dared
First in the battle to strive and sorrow
Scorned, spurned, naught have ye cared!
Raising your eyes to a wider tomorrow."

"Firm in reliance, laugh a defiance,
Laugh in hope, for sure is the end.

"March, march, many as one!
Shoulder to shoulder, and friend to friend!"

*E*thel's music
didn't stop there.

Like a steady breeze,
"March of the Women"
traveled across land ...

...and ocean...

...to places near...

...and far.

Ethel's music marches on. Shoulder to shoulder, friend to friend, women the world over dare to march, sing, and dream of equality...

...today,
...tomorrow,
...and forever.

More About Ethel Smyth

Ethel Smyth's contemporaries are household names—Johannes Brahms, Peter Ilyich Tchaikovsky, and Edvard Grieg, to name a few. Although Ethel's works were highly regarded during her lifetime, her music has been overlooked in history, solely because of her gender.

Ethel left her career as a composer for two years to join the suffragettes. Emmeline Pankhurst, leader of the Women's Social and Political Union, was Ethel's close friend. Together, they worked tirelessly for women's suffrage in Britain. After serving her prison sentence at Holloway Prison, Ethel returned to composing full-time.

In 1920, Ethel began to lose her hearing and eventually had to give up composing music. She became an author and published ten books about her musical life and her time as a suffragette.

"The exact worth of my music will probably not be known till naught remains of the author but sexless dots and lines on ruled paper."
—Ethel Smyth

Timeline of Ethel's Musical Life

1858: Ethel Smyth was born in Kent, England, to General and Mrs. Smyth. The family moved to Frimley, England, in 1867 when General Smyth was appointed Commander of Artillery at Aldershot.

1870: Ethel became enamored with classical music at the age of 12 when she heard her governess, who had attended Leipzig Conservatory of Music, play Beethoven sonatas on the piano.

1872: At age 14, Ethel began studying the music and lives of great composers on her own. She began to experiment with writing her own music, set to poetry. Against the wishes of her parents, Ethel became obsessed with the goal of someday attending Leipzig Conservatory to study composition.

1877: Ethel entered Leipzig Conservatory and became the student of Carl Reinecke, Salomon Jadassohn and Louis Maas. Here she worked with Tchaikovsky, Grieg, and Dvořák. Ethel left the conservatory after a year to take lessons with composer Heinrich Herzogenberg and became a friend of Johannes Brahms and Clara Schumann.

1890: Ethel was named a "promising young composer" when a four-movement serenade she composed, Serenade in D, debuted at the Crystal Palace in London, England.

1891: Ethel composed Mass in D, which is regarded as one of her most important works.

Critics compared this work to Ludwig van Beethoven's *Missa solemnis*.

1898: Ethel's first opera, *Fantasio*, premiered in Wiemar, Germany.

1902: Ethel's second opera, *Der Wald*, premiered at the Royal Opera in Berlin, Germany. This opera became the first opera by a woman to be performed at the Metropolitan Opera House in New York in March 1903.

1906: Ethel's third opera, *The Wreckers*, debuted in Liepzig, Germany, and Prague, Czech Republic. This opera is now considered to be Ethel's masterpiece.

1910: Ethel was awarded an honorary doctorate degree from the University of Durham in Durham, England.

1910: Ethel became friends with Emmeline Pankhurst, leader of the Women's Social and Political Union, and stopped her composing career to join the suffragette movement in Britain.

1911: Ethel wrote the music to "March of the Women." Cicely Hamilton, a fellow suffragette, wrote the lyrics. The song became an anthem of the suffragette movement. Suffragettes marched and sang the song as they fought for the right to vote. The song was published in pamphlets and given out at women's marches and rallies in Britain and beyond.

ETHEL WITH HER BELOVED DOG, MARCO

1912: Ethel served two months in Holloway Prison for throwing a rock through a cabinet minister's window. While visiting Holloway Prison, conductor Thomas Beecham (1879–1961) witnessed Ethel Smyth conducting "March of the Women" with her toothbrush from her prison cell as women in the prison courtyard gathered below to sing and march.

1914–16: Ethel returned to her career as a composer and continued to compose, producing yet another opera, *The Boatswain's Mate*.

1920-21: Ethel began to lose her hearing, making it difficult for her to compose.

1922: For her contributions to music, Ethel was named a British dame, the feminine version of knighthood.

1930: Despite hearing loss, Ethel composed her choral symphony *The Prison*.

1944: Ethel died at the age of 86, leaving behind a wealth of musical masterpieces.

PIANO

- Sonata No. 1 in C (1877)
- *Variations on an Original Theme (of an Exceedingly Dismal Nature) in D-flat* (1878)
- Prelude and Fugue in F-sharp (1880)
- *Prelude and Fugue for Thin People* (1883)

ORGAN

- *Fugue á 5* (1882)
- *Short Chorale Preludes* (1882)
- *Prelude on a Traditional Irish Air* (1938)

ORCHESTRAL WORKS

- Serenade in D (1889)
- Overture to Shakespeare's *Antony and Cleopatra* (1889)
- Suite For Strings, Op. 1A (1891)
- *Four Short Chorale Preludes for Strings and Solo Instruments* (1913)

Selected List of Amazing Music by Ethel Smyth

OPERA

- *Fantasio* (1898)
- *Der Wald* (1902)
- *The Wreckers* (1906)
- *The Boatswain's Mate* (1916)
- *Fête Galante* (1923)
- *Entente Cordiale* (1925)

CHORAL

- "Lieder" with piano, Op. 4 (1877)
- "Lieder und Balladen" (1886)
- "The Song of Love," Op. 8 (1888)
- Mass in D (1891)
- "Hey Nonny No" for choir and orchestra (1911)
- "The March of the Women" (lyrics by Cicely Hamilton) (1911)
- "Moods of the Sea" (1913)
- *The Prison*, cantata for soprano, bass, choir, and orchestra (1930)

CHAMBER MUSIC

- Sonata for cello and piano in C minor (1880)
- Trio for violin, cello, and piano in D minor (1880)
- String Quartet in D minor (1880)
- String Quartet in C minor (1883)
- String Quintet in E, Op. 1 (1883)

CONCERTO

- Concerto for violin and horn in A (1926)

BRASS

- *Hot Potatoes* (1930)

Sources

Collis, Lousie. *Impetuous Heart*. London: William Kimber & Co. Limited, 1984.

"Ethel Smyth." Brooklyn Museum: Ethel Smyth, n.d. https://www.brooklynmuseum.org/eascfa/dinner_party/place_settings/ethel_smyth.

"Ethel Smyth: The March of the Women." British Library, n.d. https://www.bl.uk/collection-items/smyth-march-of-the-women.

Gale Primary Sources, British Library Newspapers. "Conducted In Prison With Toothbrush: British Lady Composer Dead." *Dundee Courier* (Dundee, Scotland) Wednesday, May 10, 1944. Issue 28372

Gale Primary Sources, British Library Newspapers. "The Only Safe Source of Happiness by Dame Ethel Smyth." *Evening Telegraph* (Dundee, Scotland) Monday, November 15, 1937. Issue 19024

Gale Primary Sources, British Library Newspapers. "The Window Breakers." *Exeter and Plymouth Gazette* (Exeter, England) Volume CXL, Issue 20369.

Gates, Eugene. "Dame Ethel Smyth: Pioneer of English Opera," *The Kapralova Society Journal, A Journal Of Women In Music*, Volume II, Issue I, Spring 2013. http://www.kapralova.org/journal20.pdf

Sadie, Julie Anne, and Samuel Rhian, eds. *The Norton/Grove Dictionary of Women Composers*. W.W. Norton & Company, 1995: 429-433.

Smyth, Ethel. *Impressions That Remained, Volume I*. New Edition. London: Longmans, Green & Co, New York, Toronto, Bombay, Calcutta and Madras, 1923.

Smyth, Ethel. "The March of the Women: Dedicated to the Women's Social and Political Union." (song) 1911, by Ethel Smyth. Lyrics by Cicely Hamilton.

Smyth, Ethel. *What Happened Next (Ethel Smyth to Henry Brewster, 1902)* London: Longmans, Green & Co. New York, Toronto, Bombay, Calcutta and Madras, 1940. 210.

Smyth, Ethel, and Cicely Hamilton. "Image 2 of Songs of Sunrise Choral Group. No. 3, The March of the Women : for Mixed Chorus and Band (in G) ; Issued Also in Popular Edition (in F)." Library of Congress, n.d. https://www.loc.gov/resource/mussuffrage.mussuffrage-100005/?sp=2.

Wood, Elizabeth. "On Deafness and Musical Creativity: The Case of Ethel Smyth." *The Musical Quarterly* 92, no. 1/2 (2009): 33-69. Accessed November 2, 2020. http://www.jstor.org/stable/27751853.

Zigler, Amy. "Biography." Dame Ethel Smyth, n.d. https://www.ethelsmyth.org/about/biography/.

Zigler, Amy Elizabeth. "Selected Chamber Works of Dame Ethel Smyth; A Dissertation Presented To The Graduate School Of The University of Florida In Partial Fulfillment Of The Requirements For The Degree Of Doctor Of Philosophy, University of Florida." UF George A. Smathers Libraries, 2009. Accessed 3/25/21. https://ufdc.ufl.edu/UFE0041106/00001

"I feel I must fight for my music, because I want women to turn their minds to big and difficult jobs; not just to go on hugging the shore, afraid to be put out to sea."
—Ethel Smyth

About the Creators

Diane Worthey is an author and musician. Her works include *In One Ear & Out the Other: Antonia Brico & Her Amazingly Musical Life*, which was a 2020 Junior Library Guild Gold Standard Selection and won the first place 2021 Paterson Prize for Young Readers in Grades 4–6. In addition to writing books for children with classical music themes, Diane is a classically trained violinist and performs in the Washington–Idaho Symphony. She also teaches violin and viola to all ages of budding musicians at the University of Idaho Preparatory Division in Moscow, Idaho. Visit her at dianeworthey.blog.

Helena Pérez García is a Spanish illustrator whose work has appeared across magazines, newspapers, packaging, and books for children and adults internationally. Her illustrations are conceptual, whimsical, and rich in detail and color. Helena's primary medium is gouache, and her main sources of inspiration are art, literature, and cinema. Some of her clients include Penguin Random House, The Body Shop, Tate Publishing, *The Financial Times*, *Reader's Digest*, and *Il Corriere della Sera*, among many others.

If you liked this book, please leave a review online at your favorite retailer. Honest reviews spread the word about Bushel & Peck—and help us make better books, too!

www.bushelandpeckbooks.com/pages/nominate-a-school-or-organization

About Bushel & Peck Books

Bushel & Peck Books is a children's publishing house with a special mission. Through our Book-for-Book Promise™, we donate one book to kids in need for every book we sell.

Ethel's Music Lives On

After nearly eighty years since Ethel's death in 1944, audiences the world over are now rediscovering her remarkable music. In 2019, under the direction of James Blachly and Steven Fox, the Experiential Orchestra and Chorus featuring soloists Sarah Brailey and Dashon Burton recorded Ethel Smyth's *The Prison* with producer Blanton Alspaugh and Soundmirror recording company. The recording was released on Chandos Records in 2020 in both the UK and the United States. In 2021, the recording won a GRAMMY® Award for Best Classical Solo Vocal Album. For more information about this groundbreaking recording of Ethel Smyth's *The Prison*, please visit experientialorchestra.com/smyth.

JAMES BLACHLY

THE EXPERIENTIAL ORCHESTRA AND CHORUS

"As I discovered when I first encountered her superb compositions, Ethel Smyth's music speaks for itself. But reading about her remarkable life story can also compel us to do more—to be more bold and to fight for what we believe in. Told here in a wonderful way by Diane Worthey, this book will inspire people of all ages and genders." —James Blachly